# HOW TO DRAW BOOK FOR CHILDREN LEARNING IS FUN EDITION

# How to use the book

. . .

Copy the simple steps on the blank page to Learn how to draw the animal or object!

# This Book Belongs to

______________________________

# Draw the Playful Kitty

# Sketch Here

# Draw Curious Mrs. Cow

# Sketch Here

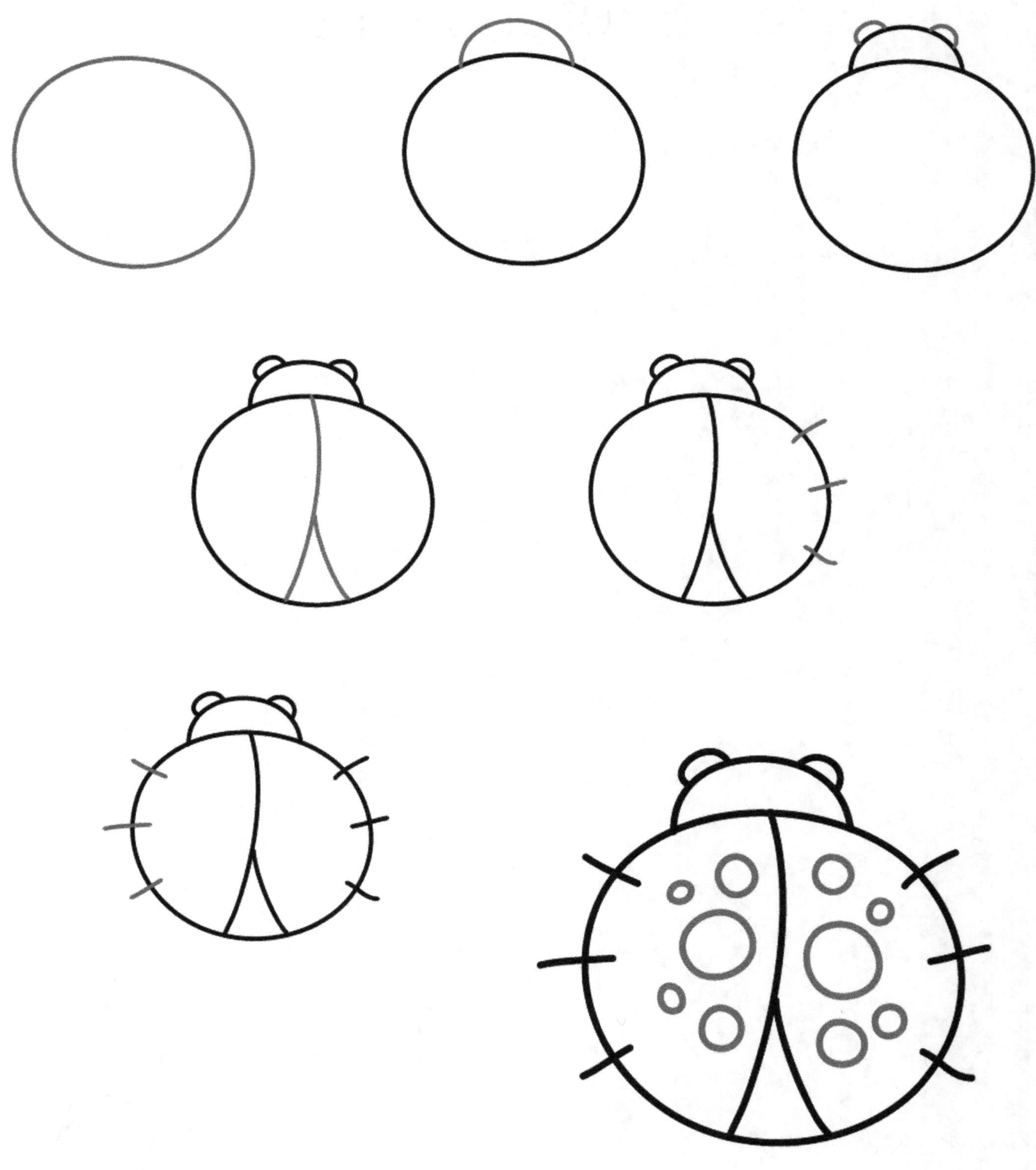

# Draw the Ladybug

# Sketch Here

# Draw the Ninja

# Sketch Here

# Draw the Rabbit

# Sketch Here

# Draw the Lucky Leprechaun

# Sketch Here

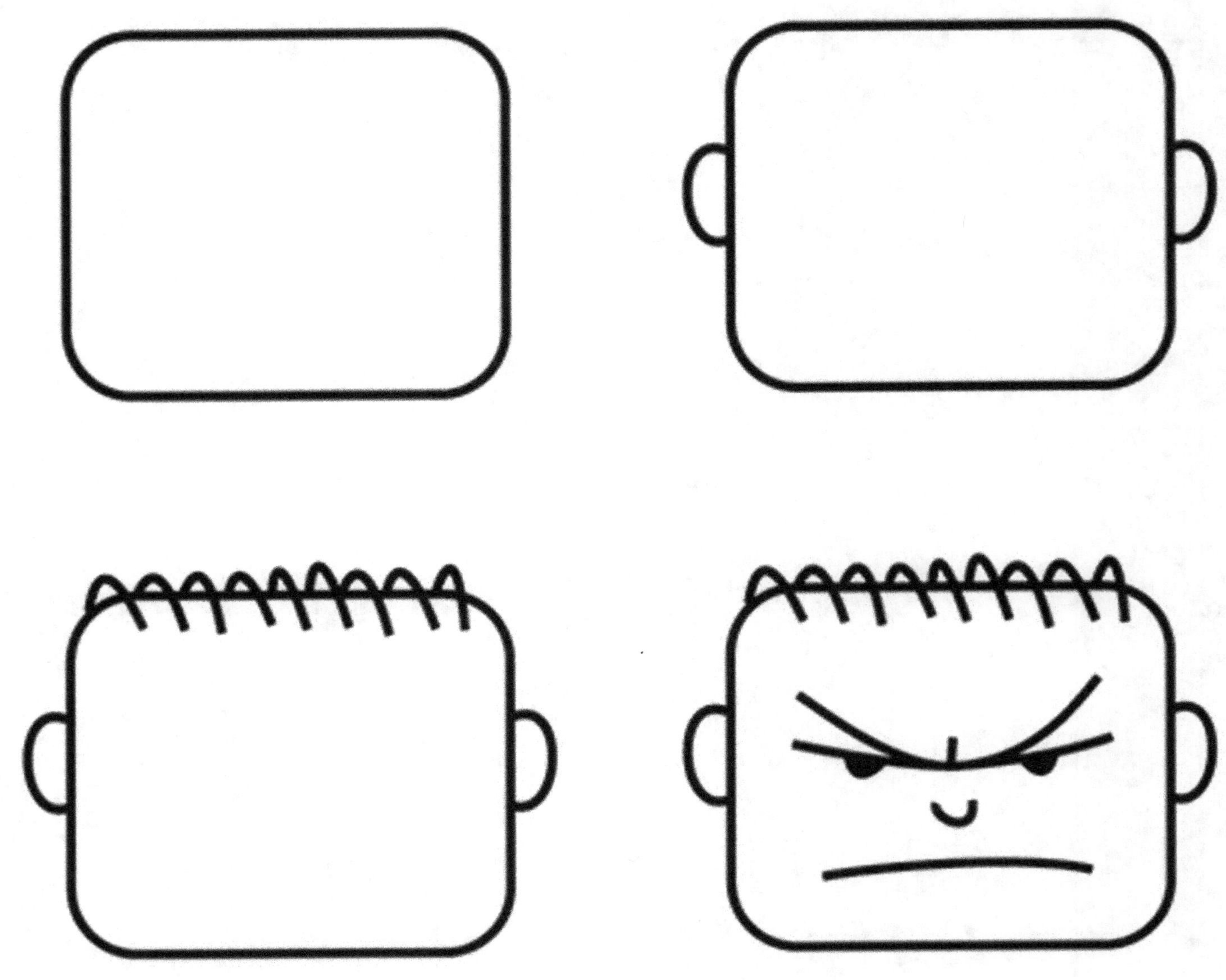

# Draw the Angry Man's Face

# Sketch Here

# Draw the Bus

# Sketch Here

# Draw the Space Alien

# Sketch Here

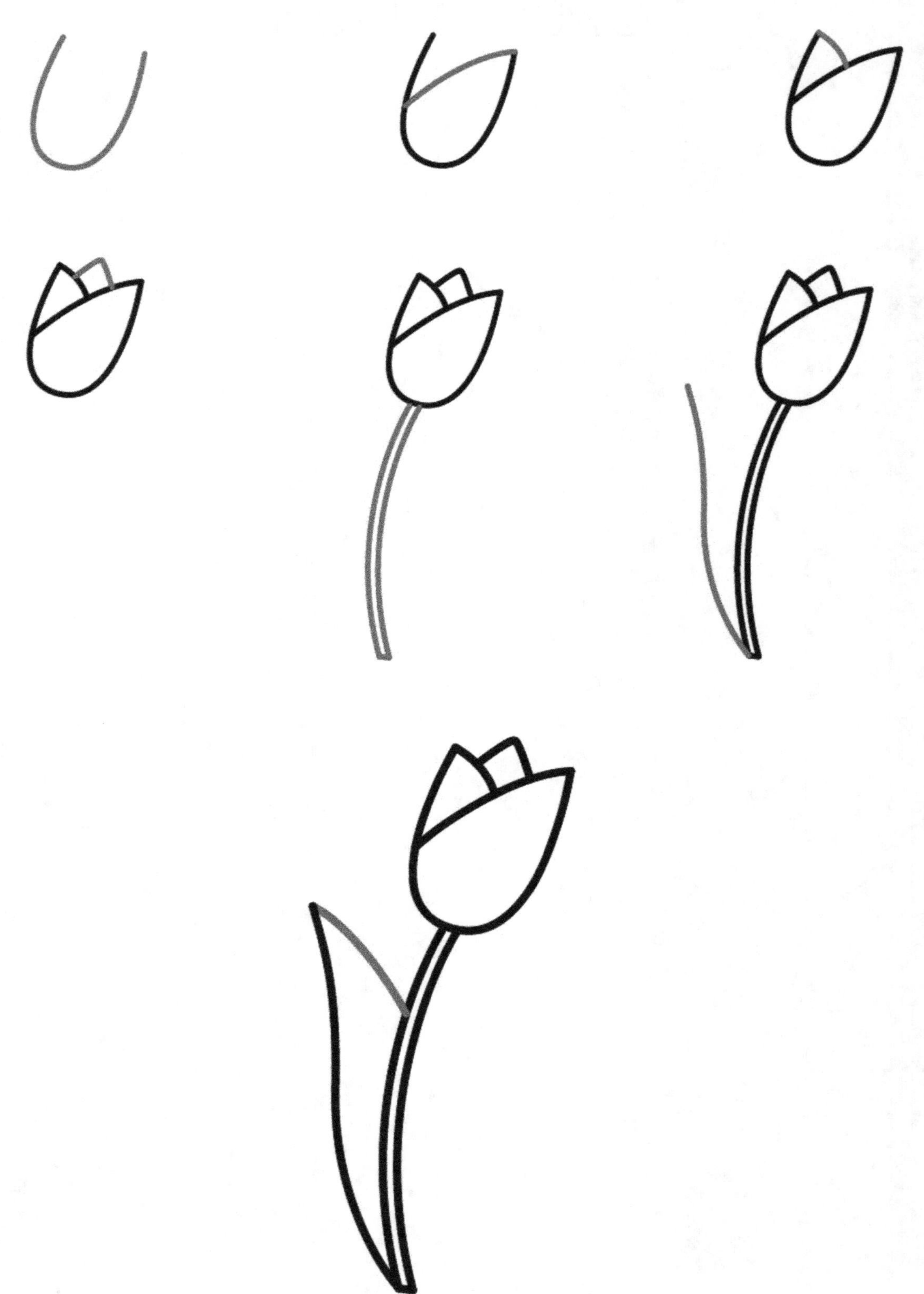

# Draw the Pretty Tulips

# Sketch Here

# Draw the Halloween Bat

# Sketch Here

# Draw the Cute Mouse

# Sketch Here

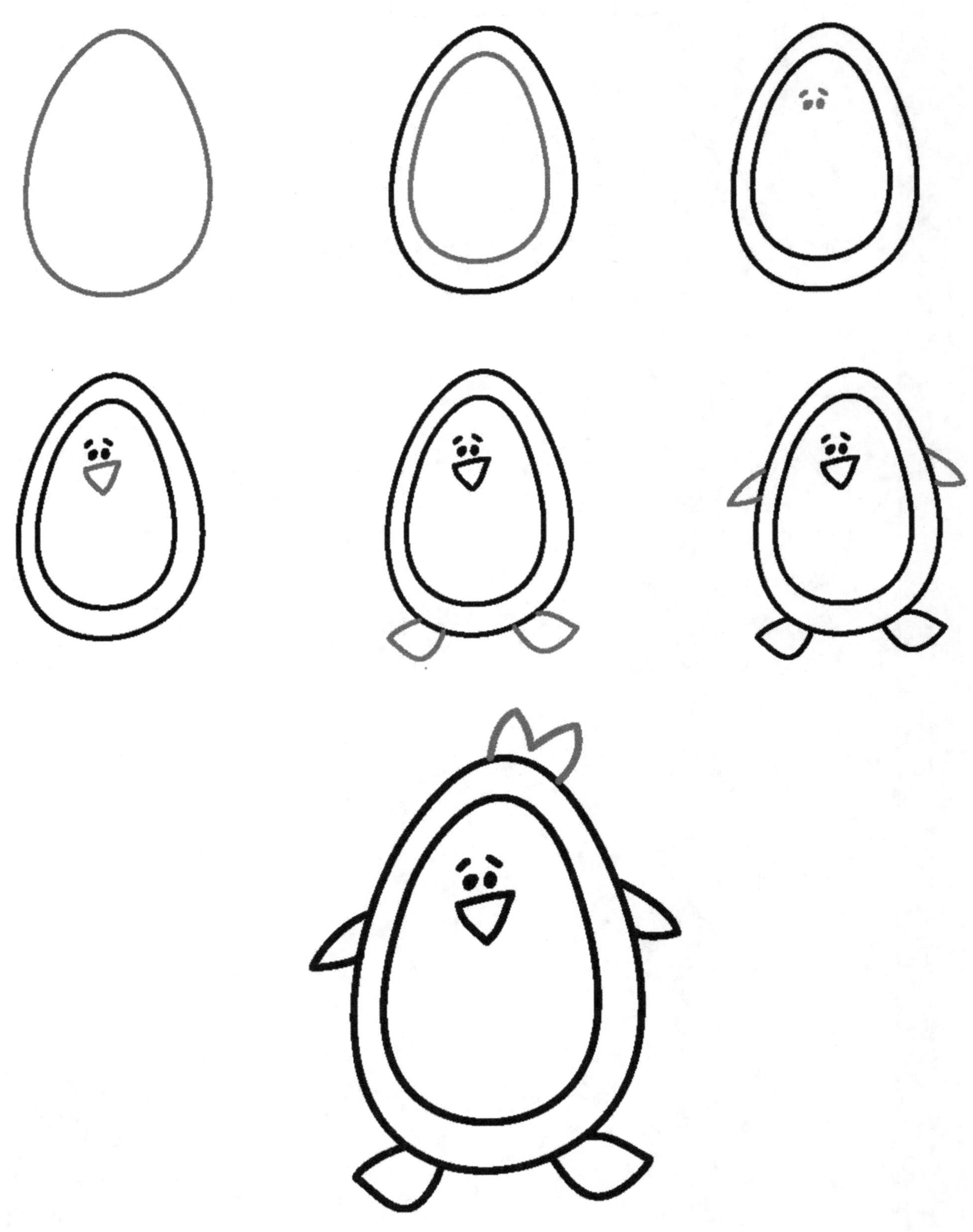

# Draw the Pretty Penguin

# Sketch Here

Draw the Gleeful Face

# Sketch Here

# Draw the Little Duckling

# Sketch Here

# Draw the Sheep

# Sketch Here

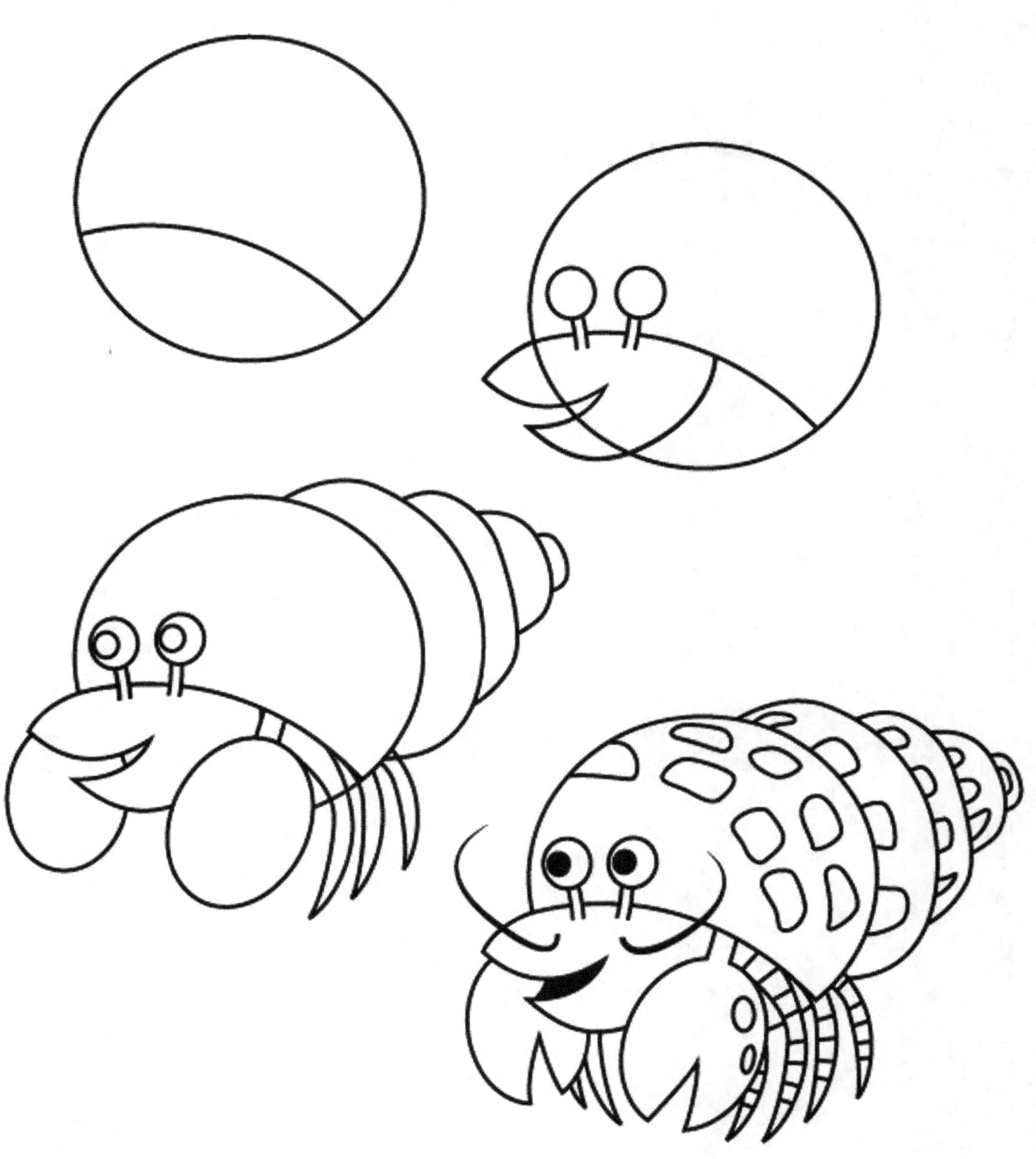

# Draw the Hermit Crab

# Sketch Here

# Draw the Scarecrow

# Sketch Here

# Draw the Reindeer

# Sketch Here

# Draw Mr. Billy Goat

# Sketch Here

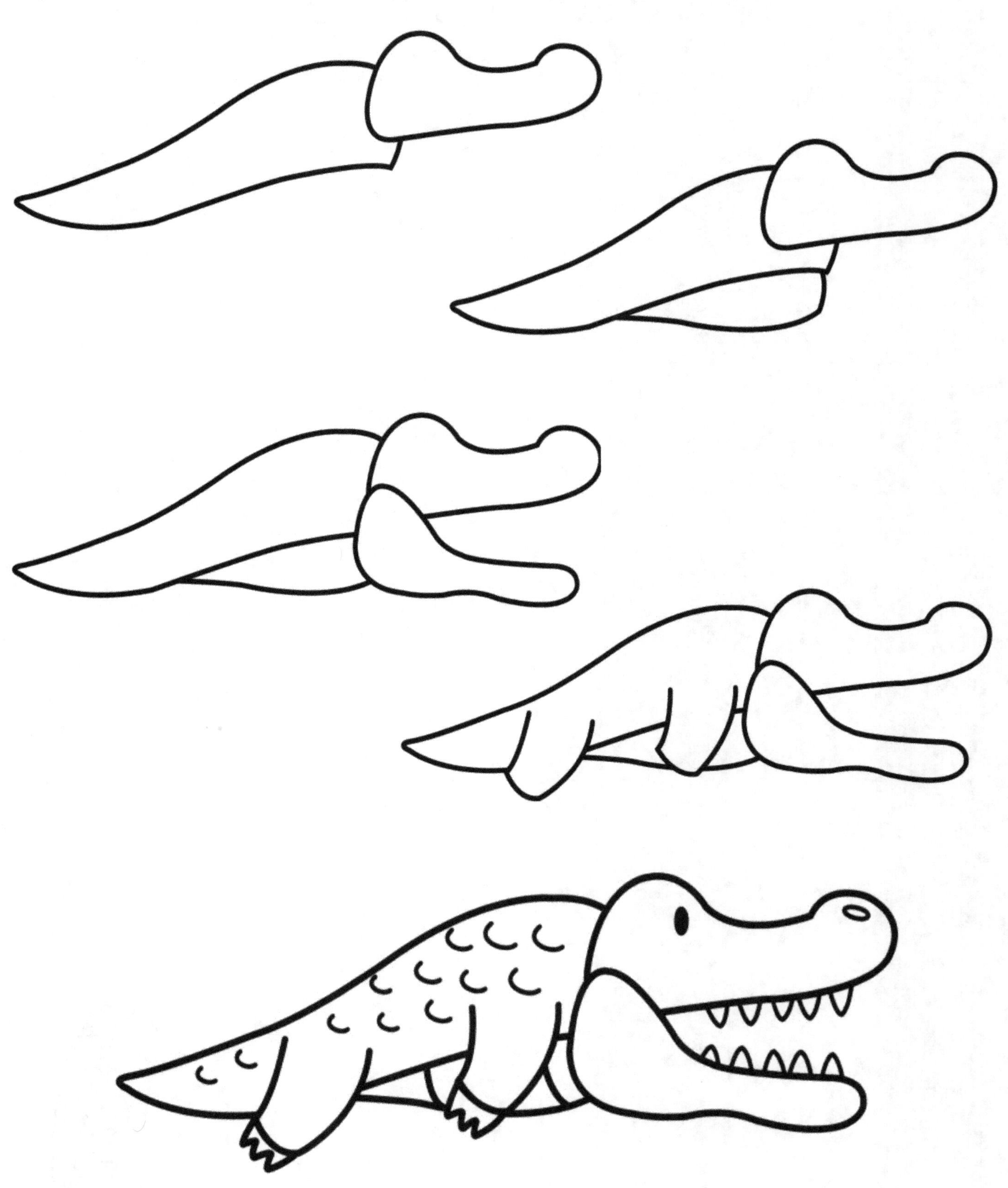

# Draw Mr. Crocodile

# Sketch Here

# Draw the Mother Hen

# Sketch Here

# Draw the Baby Chick

# Sketch Here

www.ingramcontent.com/pod-product-compliance
Lightning Source LLC
LaVergne TN
LVHW082301150826
845677LV00009B/1680
* 9 7 9 8 8 6 9 4 5 3 6 4 8 *